My Grandmother is always with me

A Remembering Journey

Written by Lorraine Hedtke & Addison Yost
Illustration by Annette Olson & Addison Yost
Includes: A Grown Up Guide to Remembering

To order additional copies of this book, contact:
Xlibris
1-888-795-4274
www.Xlibris.com
Orders@Xlibris.com

www.rememberingpractices.com

ISBN: 978-1-4134-8776-3 (sc)

Library of Congress Control Number: 2005901490

Print information available on the last page

Rev. date: 04/08/2020

Even though she died long before I was born, she has always been an important person in my life.

My Grandmother was a bright and happy person.
She taught me to look for the best in people.

5

I imagine she's sending me a spectrum of colors and watching over me.

My Grandmother loved the beauty of nature. I remember this every time I see a rainbow or a colorful sunset.

Sometimes, I remember her when the sun breaks through
the clouds in gold shimmering light.

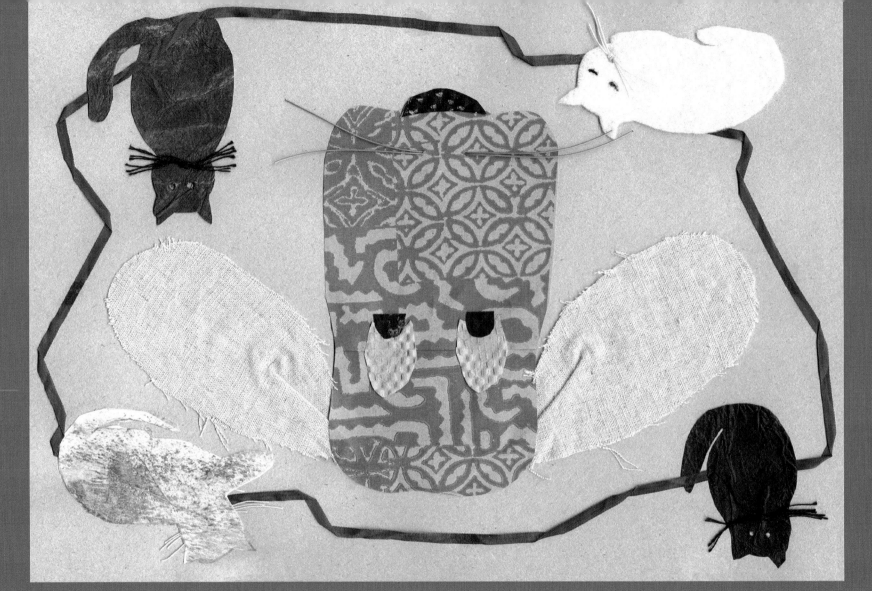

She is always with me when I am with animals. My Grandmother loved animals as much as I do. When I was eight, I got my first dog, Zealand. I also have two cats named Rocket and Starlight. I promised my Mom to help look after the animals by feeding them and playing with them. I trained my dog to do all kinds of tricks. I imagine that my Grandmother would be happy if she was to see me play with them.

She would know how happy they make me. I can think of her when I am with them. I know she would be proud of me for how I am with them.

Where I live, an owl visits me often. It has a nest out front my house.
My Grandmother especially liked owls.

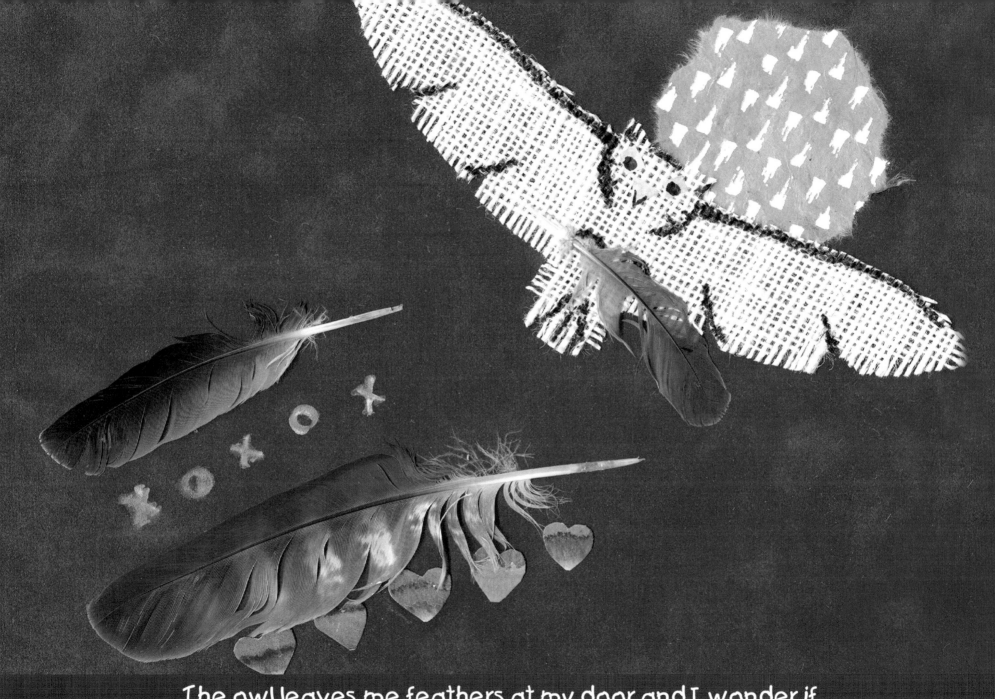

The owl leaves me feathers at my door and I wonder if they are messages from my Grandmother.

When I hear the owl's nightsong, my Grandmother's wise advice lives on in its sweet hooting. I imagine the owl can carry my message to her.

On my 6th birthday, I thought my Grandmother was singing me a birthday song.
My Mom and I have sung her songs since I was a little kid.
They always help me snuggle into sleep.

It's a gift, simple
to be a gift.

I like hearing her favorite songs. I like having my Mom sing them to me. Sometimes, when we are at church, we will sing a song that I know she liked.

My Grandmother loved classical music. When I was eight, I started playing piano.
I know she would be happy that I play the piano.

My first recital was on my Grandmother's piano. It felt like she was guiding my fingers as I played for everyone. I know she would have been the loudest one clapping after I played my song!

I remember my Grandmother every breakfast!

My Mom makes me my *favorite* pancakes from Grandmom's recipes. My tummy stays full and warm all morning.

Someday, I will make Grandmom's pancakes for my kids.
I hope they will like knowing Grandmother like I do.

I have seen places she liked and imagined how her eyes saw things.
She loved the way the desert looked in the spring, when the flowers bloomed.

She loved the different colors of the wild desert flowers.

21

I like to wear some of her jewelry and imagine what it felt like on her when she wore it. When my Mom got married, I wore my Grandmother's garnet ring and bracelet. I loved wearing something of hers especially because I know she wore them at her wedding too a long time ago.

People tell me stories about her. My uncle has told me how Grandmom liked to joke and have fun. He likes to tell funny stories about her. He says it helps him remember her.

Looking at pictures lets me see what she looked like. I notice how she and I look alike in pictures. My eyes and eyebrows look just like hers. And my lips have the same heart shape to them that she had.

When I was born, I had a special pink birthmark on my leg.
Mom and I decided that this must be Grandmother's lipstick
from kissing me. We always called it my strawberry kiss.

I like to introduce people to my Grandmother. I like to tell people who didn't get the chance to know her all about her. I have told my Mom's husband about her. It was nice to tell him how she liked animals like I do.

My Grandmother helped many people when she was alive.
I hope her stories will still help others, like they have helped me.
She had a big heart and was kind to people.
Her memory reminds me that I have a big heart too.

My Grandmother is always with me...

Guiding me ...Teaching me ...Protecting me ...Loving me.

A Grown Up Guide To Remembering
Written by Lorraine Hedtke MSW, ACSW, LCSW

Children look to us as adults to guide and assist them through the confusing time both before and after the death of a loved one. This brief explanation is intended as a resource for adults to help you answer children's questions and reassure their uncertainties. We want to give you a few ideas to assist you to guide your children during these important times. With these suggestions, our children can be helped to actively remember their deceased loved ones, rather than dwell only on the pain of loss. Through remembering, children can honor the relationship they have with their dead loved ones in ways that enrich their own and their family's lives. We hope that this guide will spark ideas and practices that invite the joyful moments of remembering with your children.

Death, Grief and Children

When a loved one dies, children are often left with many questions. It is quite possible that a child might ask about the meaning of death or where their loved one has gone. Children may be left with unanswered questions, feelings and thoughts that they don't have a vocabulary to express. The time after a person dies can be confusing for young children and they need grown up help to make sense out of the situation.

In the recent past, children were often overlooked when a person died. Under the pretext of protecting children's feelings, parents have often excluded children from experiencing and responding to death and bereavement. It is still not uncommon for children to not be allowed to visit their dying loved one in a hospital for fear that it might be too traumatic. Children, too, have been often kept from attending funerals and memorial services for those whom they love. The result has been a general silencing of discussion of the grief or sadness that a child might feel after a death of a person, or a pet, whom they loved.

In recent years, however, adults have been guided by a different set of social and emotional rules in their own experience of grief. People are often hurried through mourning. They are expected to "move on" and resume "normal life", sometimes with undue haste. Feelings other than sadness might even be frowned upon. In efforts to "get over their death", stories are not shared and relationships with the deceased get buried. It has not been uncommon for these ways of behaving to be overlaid upon a child's experience as well.

The Birth of My Grandmother Is Always With Me

Addison and her grandmother have enjoyed a loving connection over the years. We like to think that Addison's Grandmother has been with her from her own birth, 13 years ago, and will be with her for the rest of Addison's life. My mother's narratives provide congruent connection with Addison's past and to values that may serve her in the years to come. This connection gives Addison a place of belonging in the world and can guide her at times when life seems challenging. Not only is Addison the beneficiary of this connection, but those who come to know Addison's Grandmother, through Addison's stories, reap the benefits as well.

In this instance, Addison's grandmother died fifteen years before her birth. We have brought her grandmother's life into focus through various remembering practices, as can be heard in how Addison tells of her. The story that is told here is their story of connection, relationship and love.

A New Approach to Death and Grief

This book offers an example of a different approach to death. When a loved one dies, our love for them does not die. We still love that person as we did before, but we now need to use our memories more deliberately to keep this love alive. What's more, we need to speak about, and act

upon, what we remember in order for it to continue to have significance in our own lives. This is true for adults and children alike. The wonderful memories that we once shared do not need to be tucked away in an attic trunk alongside our favorite photograph. We can spend time remembering, and sharing together, the special times we shared with our loved one, the stories that they told us, and their words of encouragement. The remembered love that a deceased person showed us can continue to be a wonderful resource in our lives. Its influence does not need to end with death. When we think in this way, we are then free to keep, and grow, these memories for the rest of our lives. We can look for guidance and comfort from loved ones in the process of remembering them. There is no need to say goodbye to the dead. We believe it is better to keep them alive through remembering.

Conversations and practices that invite remembering help to establish positive relationships even with those who have been deceased for many years, as with Addison and her Grandmother. These conversations can also help children when the death of a person that they knew well has occurred more recently. Conversations that affirm ongoing relationship in these instances can nurture hope in times that might appear bleak. Remembering helps children make sense of these times.

Children particularly enjoy remembering. When asked about what was important to them about their deceased father or mother or grandparent, they are ever ready with information. It does not take much prodding for a child to bring to life the voice of a deceased loved one. Just as when a child speaks through the voice of a stuffed animal, he or she can easily materialize the stories they shared with those who have died. In this way, remembering can continue to be a resource and place of comfort. Forgetting is not necessary.

This approach contrasts with the idea that a child should be helped to face the harsh reality of loss and should learn not to think about their loved one as still alive. This emphasis requires a child to forget that the deceased person was an important part of this person's life.

When children are encouraged to remember and share their special stories, they continue to develop a connection with the person who has died. They might say that they feel as though their deceased mother or sibling or grandparent is a guardian angel who offers them protection in a big and scary world. Or, they might sense that their deceased pet or father or friend whispered words of encouragement to them at times of struggle and hardship.

How We Remember Matters

Remembering is not intended as a catalyst for a child to 'get more in touch with his or her sadness'. After the death of a loved one, it is normal and understandable for a child to feel sad when someone they love has died. Children need comfort and support when they feel sad. However, sadness is only one aspect of the complexity of grief. Rather than encouragement to feel these feelings more intensely, remembering helps them manage the sadness effectively. We suggest that the relationship with the deceased loved one after death can continue to reflect the many tones and textures that were available to us while the person was alive.

The art of remembering selects the most positive aspects of a relationship for focus. It can continue to develop over many years. In the process it can help shape the child's personal development. Accessing stories of strength and appreciation help build a child's strengths and character. If we ask children to focus on the affirming aspects of relationship, they will incorporate joy, pride, and personal satisfaction. Listening to their stories about their deceased loved ones can also lead us as parents to notice and appreciate moments of accomplishment or character in our children. In these ways, remembering brings the best of the past into the promise of a positive future.

How to Use This Book

We invite you to use these practices as a guide. Read the book with your children and speak about points of similarity in their experience. For example, discuss the times and places that your child feels the connection and love of your loved one who has died. Ask them whether there are rituals and practices they would like to develop to connect with a dead loved one? Who might they share these practices with? Are there reminders of this person that are pleasurable to keep close? What stories do they remember about the person who has died? What might the person who has died say about how your child is doing with school or friends? How does your children want to continue to hear their loved one's voice and recall their presence? What do they like about remembering?

We encourage you to speak often with your children about your loved one who has died. Continue to explore with them what is helpful to recall. Through these conversations, the relationship with the loved one can continue to be a resource and a place of comfort. Over the years, the memories can grow and take different shape as the child grows. Rather than thinking that our love will fade with time, remembering can allow the connection to continue to grow.

An Invitation

We welcome your special stories of remembering. We have established a website where stories of love, connection and relationship can be shared. Should you and your child like to contribute your stories, they would be most welcome. This offers another place too where your loved ones can continue to live and inspire others.

www.rememberingpractices.com

About Lorraine

Lorraine Hedtke has studied narrative therapy and social constructionism since 1988. She has taught her unique philosophy about death, dying and bereavement at hospices, universities and private agencies in the United States, New Zealand, Australia and England. Lorraine's ideas are distinctive and represent a departure from standard theories of grief. Articles about her work have appeared in numerous international professional journals and newspapers. Her book for professional audiences, co-authored with John Winslade, *Remembering Lives: Conversations with The Dying and The Bereaved* (2004, Baywood Publishing) provides a new and innovative way to understand death and grief. She lives in Southern California and is employed by VITAS Innovative Hospice Care as a Bereavement Services Manager. Lorraine shares her life with her wonderful daughter, incredible husband and the thousands of stories from those who are no longer living.

Writing this book with Addison and Annette has been a delight to see her mother's life continue to touch and inspire and fill us with love. Lorraine lives her belief, "Our lives are not inconsequential."

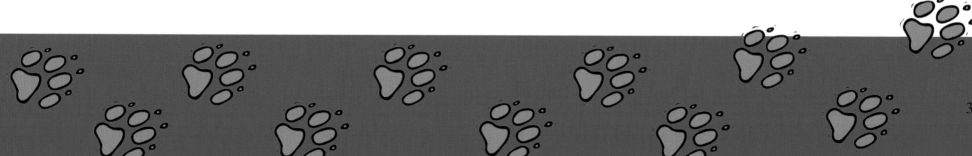

About Addison

Besides her connection with her grandmother, Addison shares her daily life with her many animals. She is almost thirteen now. For years, she has been interested in art and music. To create the illustrations for this book, she worked with Annette to make many of the collages.

When Addie is not doing her homework, she is enjoying the activities that come with being an active sixth grade student. She plays the piano with gusto, and loves to play her drums. In her spare time, she enjoys playing volleyball and chatting on the computer to friends. She dreams of being an architect someday to build beautiful houses and having a farm with horses.

About Annette

Annette Olson is a native of Wisconsin and has been painting in various media since the 1970's. She has studied watercolor, drawing, acrylic and collage techniques through workshops and classes and is currently focusing on collage. Since moving to Arizona 8 years ago, she has shown her work in several galleries, juried shows. While living in Tucson, she became a juried member of the Southern Arizona Watercolor Guild and The Collage Association. Recently, Annette won the 2005 poster and publicity contest for The Mountain Artist Guild in Prescott Arizona. Her collage, *Just Jugs* will be used for tee-shirts and publicity for the group for 2005.

Annette's cat, Charlie, and her dog, Dickens, gave her many ideas for the collage pictures in this book. Every once in a while, Charlie helped by walking through the wet paint and Dickens helped choose some words for the pictures. Annette said, "It has been exciting to create the art for this special book. I loved discovering just the right collage piece for the image that the words suggest".

She hopes to continue illustrating children's books.

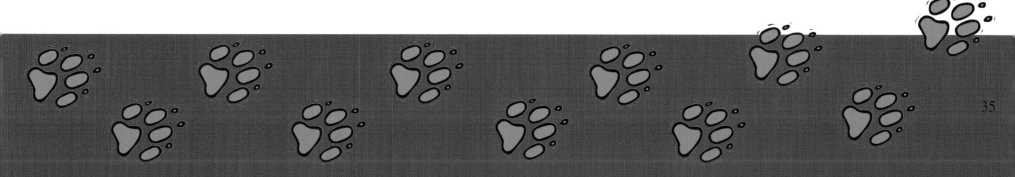

Printed in the United States
By Bookmasters